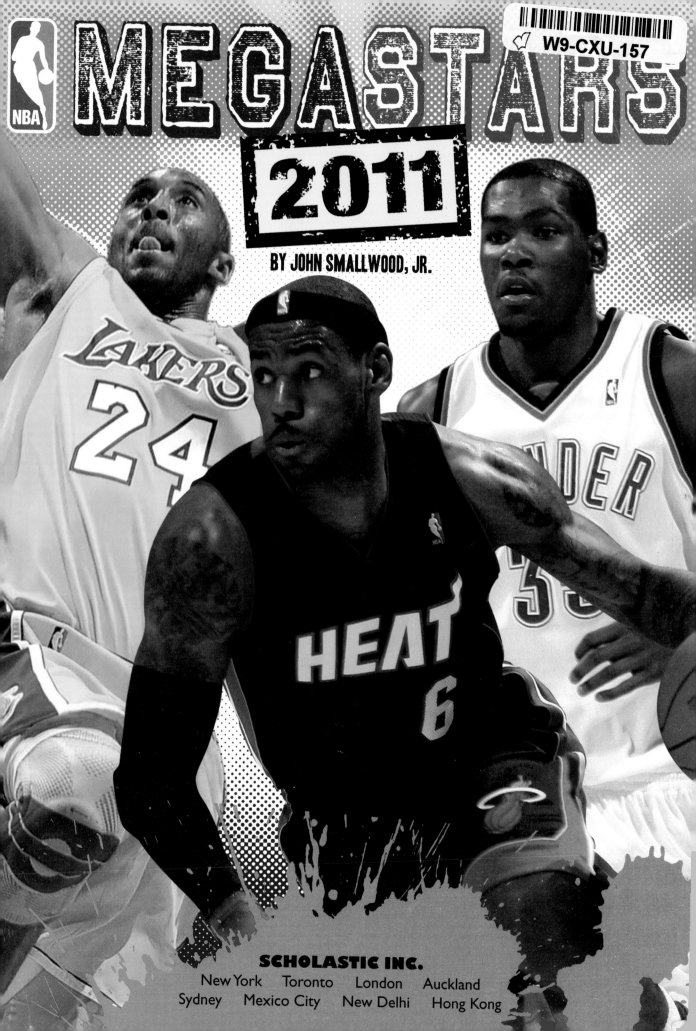

Cover and title page: (left) Andrew D Berstein/NBAE/Getty Images; (center) Scott Cunningham/NBAE/Getty Images; (right) Layne Murdoch/NBAE/Getty Images

Interior: (3 top left) © Danny Bollinger/NBAE/Getty Images; (3 top middle, 30 middle) © Noah Graham/NBAE/Getty Images; (3 top right, 29) © Nathaniel S Butler/NBAE/Getty Images; (3 bottom left, 21) © Barry Gossage/NBAE/Getty Images; (4 top left, 7) © Scott Cunningham/NBAE/Getty Images; (4 top right) © Larry W Smith/NBAE/Getty Images; (4 bottom left) © David Liam Kyle/NBAE/Getty Images; (4 middle bottom) © Issac Baldizon/NBAE/Getty Images; (4 bottom right, 13, 30 right) © Fernando Medina/NBAE/Getty Images; (5 top left & top middle) © Andrew D Bernstein/NBAE/Getty Images; (5 top left) © Christian Peterson/Getty Images; (5 bottom; 9; 30 left) © Layne Murdoch/NBAE/Getty Images; (5) © Gary Dineen/NBAE/Getty Images; (11) © Jesse D Garrabrant/NBAE/Getty Images; (15) © Glenn James/NBAE/Getty Images; (17) © Melissa Majchrzak/NBAE/Getty Images; (19) © Brian Babineau/NBAE/Getty Images; (23) © Harry How/Getty Images; (25) © Randy Belice/NBAE/Getty Images; (27) © Joe Murphy/NBAE/Getty Images

ISBN 978-0-545-27960-4

12 11 10 9 8 7 6 5 4 3 2 1   11 12 13 14 15 16/0

Printed in the U.S.A. 40
First printing, January 2011

THEY ARE THE GREATEST ATHLETES OF THEIR ERA.

The National Basketball Association is a league of speed, agility, grace, and power. The amazing athleticism of NBA players is a wonder to watch and will always cause you to ask, "How did they do that?"

It could be Los Angeles Lakers and five-time NBA champion Kobe Bryant hitting another game-winning shot at the buzzer. It might be LeBron "King" James of the Miami Heat slashing by two defenders and driving to the rim for a high-flying spectacular dunk. Or maybe it will be the outstanding combination of size, power, and quickness of Orlando Magic center Dwight Howard that makes us say, "Wow."

For more than 60 years, the players of the NBA have pushed the limits of competition and entertainment in sport. They are the best at what they do, and each generation is challenged to take the game to higher levels of thrill and excitement. To simply make it to the NBA is an outstanding achievement, but some players set themselves apart as the greatest in the game.

These players amaze us with skills and abilities that keep us on the edge of our seat.

They are the Megastars of the National Basketball Association.
Let's meet some of them.

KOBE BRYANT
GUARD
LOS ANGELES LAKERS

BORN: 8/23/1978
HEIGHT: 6-6
WEIGHT: 205 lbs
SCHOOL: Lower Merion High School

ALL-TIME NBA GREAT

At this point, it is no longer a question that Kobe Bryant is one of the greatest players in NBA History.

The question is: Will he go down as the best ever?

That's how amazing Kobe as been during his first 14 years in the NBA.

Few could have imagined how good Kobe would become when he entered the 1996 NBA Draft as an 18-year-old high school graduate. But Kobe's legacy already includes five NBA Championships, two NBA Finals MVP Awards, 12 All-Star selections, eight First-Team All-NBA selections, and eight First-Team All Defense picks.

Now 32 years old, Kobe isn't slowing down. After leading the Lakers to the last two NBA titles, he is still at the top of his game. It's been said that Kobe does more things well than any other player in the NBA.

Kobe won his first three championships when he teamed with Shaquille O'Neal, but the Lakers took a step back when O'Neal was traded in 2004. Kobe was determined to make the Lakers a champion again. In 2007-08, Kobe averaged 28.3 points, 6.3 rebounds, 5.4 assists, and 1.8 steals. He was named 2008 NBA MVP, but the Lakers lost in the Finals to the Boston Celtics.

That summer, however, Kobe helped the United States regain the gold medal at the Olympics in Beijing, China.

Gold medals are great, but Kobe desperately wanted another NBA title.

In 2009, Kobe got his wish. In the playoffs, he averaged 30.2 points, 5.5 rebounds, and 5.1 assists as the Lakers won their first championship since 2002. Last season, Kobe got revenge against the Celtics in the Finals and won his fifth title.

DID YOU KNOW? Kobe nicknamed himself "The Black Mamba" because he said he desires his basketball skills to be like that snake's ability to strike with "ninety-nine percent accuracy at maximum speed, in rapid succession."

KOBE BRYANT

LEBRON JAMES
GUARD
MIAMI HEAT

BORN: 12/30/1984
HEIGHT: 6-8
WEIGHT: 250 lbs
SCHOOL: St. Vincent-St. Mary High School

THE KING'S JOURNEY

Like King Arthur, LeBron James is on a quest.

But instead of the legendary Holy Grail, "King James" is on a mission to capture an elusive NBA Championship.

No prize, however, comes without a price.

Last summer LeBron made the difficult decision to leave his home state of Ohio and the Cleveland Cavaliers to continue his journey in South Florida with the Miami Heat.

"To win, to win now, and win in the future," James, who grew up in Akron, Ohio, said of why he left the team that had drafted him No. 1 overall in 2003. "You want to put yourself in the right position to be able to complete and accomplish the goals you set out there."

"I understand that me going down as one of the greats won't happen until I win a championship."

As an individual, LeBron as already accomplished so much. Drafted out of St. Vincent-St. Mary High School, LeBron was the NBA Rookie-of-the-Year for 2003-2004 and has won the last two Most Valuable Player Awards.

He is a six-time NBA All-Star and two-time All-Star MVP.

In 2007, he led the Cavaliers to the first NBA Finals in franchise history but lost to the San Antonio Spurs. LeBron also won a gold medal at 2008 Olympics in Beijing, China.

Still the ultimate prize has eluded "The Chosen One."

Joining with superstars Dwayne Wade and Chris Bosh in Miami, LeBron looks to fulfill his destiny and win a NBA Championship.

DID YOU KNOW? LeBron changed his jersey number from #23 to #6 out of respect for Michael Jordan. LeBron started a petition that No. 23 should not be worn by any player in honor of Michael.

LEBRON JAMES

KEVIN DURANT
FORWARD
OKLAHOMA CITY THUNDER.

BORN: **9/29/1988**
HEIGHT: **6-9**
WEIGHT: **230 lbs**
SCHOOL: **University of Texas**

INSTANT GREATNESS

Oklahoma City knew it was getting something special when the Seattle SuperSonics relocated their team for the 2008-09 NBA season. But fans of the newly named "Thunder" could not have imagined how good second-year swingman Kevin Durant would be.

The No. 3 overall pick in the 2007 Draft, Kevin hit the NBA running by averaging 20.3 points and becoming the 2008 Rookie of the Year. Still, Kevin had played only his freshman season at the University of Texas when he was named by consensus as National Player of the year.

After one season in the NBA, he was just 20 years old: His game was still developing.

In his first season in Oklahoma, Kevin broke a record by scoring 36 points in the NBA Rookie Challenge game during 2009 NBA All-Star in Phoenix. He averaged 25.3 points. In 2009-10, Kevin took his place among the greats in the NBA by averaging 30.1 points. At 21 years old, he became the youngest scoring champion in history.

Oklahoma had not been predicted to be a top team in 2009-2010, but with Kevin leading the way, the Thunder finished 50-32 and made the playoffs. Although they were heavy underdogs against the reigning champion Los Angeles Lakers, the Thunder pushed the series to six games.

Kevin showed he was ready for primetime by averaging 25.0 points and 7.7 rebounds in his first playoff appearance.

In 2009-2010, Kevin made his first All-Star team and selected as First-Team All-NBA. That summer he was named Most Valuable Player of the 2100 FIBA World Championships as he led the United States to its first world title since 1994.

DID YOU KNOW? Kevin is the only active player to score 25 or more points in 29 consecutive games.

KEVIN DURANT

DWYANE WADE
GUARD
MIAMI HEAT

BORN: 12/30/1984
HEIGHT: 6-4
WEIGHT: 220 lbs
SCHOOL: Marquette University

IT'S ALL ABOUT WINNING

Dwyane Wade could have stopped everything:

He was the superstar player of the Miami Heat.

He was the NBA Finals MVP who had led the franchise to its only championship in 2006.

Dwyane could have said, "No," when the Heat had the chance to acquire superstar free agents LeBron James and Chris Bosh.

A free agent himself, Dwayne could have moved to another team.

Instead, Dwyane welcomed LeBron and Chris joining him in South Florida.

He knew what it felt like to win a championship: He wanted to do it over and over again.

As one of the top players in the NBA, Dwyane is a perennial All-Star, but he is a team player. It bothered him that Miami had not advanced out of the first round of the playoffs since winning the title in 2006.

With LeBron coming from the Cleveland Cavaliers and Chris from the Toronto Raptors, Dwyane knows he has the opportunity to win several championships over the next few years. Some have wondered how all three stars will mesh, but Wade will make it work because he is one of the most unselfish players in the league.

As shown by his 25.4 point career average, Dwyane can score, but he has also averaged 6.6 assists in his career.

Remember: Dwyane, LeBron, and Chris were teammates on the 2008 United States Olympic team, too. And while Dwyane was the leading scorer in the tournament for the U.S.A., the only thing that mattered to him was that they won the gold medal.

DID YOU KNOW? Dwyane is well known for his charity work through his own Dwyane Wade Foundation and other organizations. He has twice been presented the NBA's Community Assist Award.

DWYANE WADE

DWIGHT HOWARD
CENTER
ORLANDO MAGIC

BORN: 12/8/1985
HEIGHT: 6-11
WEIGHT: 265 lbs
SCHOOL: SW Atlanta Christian Academy

SUPERMAN

When Dwight Howard entered the NBA, he was not Superman—the Man of Steel who soared above Metropolis. He was more like Superboy—the kid from Smallville who was still learning how to be a hero.

Dwight was just 19 when he was drafted No. 1 overall by the Orlando Magic in the 2004 Draft. Although he was close to seven feet tall, his body had not fully developed. In the NBA, he would face men who were bigger and stronger. Still, Dwight held his own as a rookie. Averaging 12 points and 10 rebounds, he became the youngest player in NBA to average a double-double.

When Dwight returned for his second season, he had added 20 pounds of muscle. Playing with more strength and confidence he increased his averages to 15.8 points and 12.5 rebounds.

He was no longer Clark Kent.

By his third season, Dwight was recognized as one of the best big men in the game. He made his first All-Star Game and scored 20 points with 12 rebounds there. The Magic also improved with their young superstar. In 2007, Orlando made the playoffs for the first times since 2003.

It was on Feb. 16, 2008 when Superman arrived.

Wearing a red cape, Dwight won the Slam Dunk Contest at All-Star Saturday Night. His amazing talents and friendly, outgoing personality has made him one of the most popular players in the NBA.

In the summer of 2008, Dwight was the starting center for the United States National Team that won the gold medal at the Beijing Olympics.

In the 2008-09 season, Dwight helped take the Magic to another level. After averaging 20.6 points, 13.8 rebounds, and 2.9 blocked shots, Dwight was just as dominating in the playoffs.

The Magic reached the NBA Finals for just the second time in franchise history but unfortunately lost to the Los Angeles Lakers.

Last season, Orlando lost to the Boston Celtics in the Eastern Conference Finals, but with Superman leading the way, the Magic are set to do great things.

DID YOU KNOW? In 2009, Dwight was one of the 10 finalists for the Jefferson Awards for Public Service, which recognizes the charitable work of athletes.

DWIGHT HOWARD

DIRK NOWITZKI
FORWARD
DALLAS MAVERICKS

BORN: **6/19/1978**
HEIGHT: **7-0**
WEIGHT: **245 lbs**

DER KAISER

It's been a long time since anyone asked why Dirk started playing basketball in his native Germany instead of the more popular sport of soccer: Dirk has been so good as an NBA player it doesn't really matter.

Drafted by the Milwaukee Bucks 9th overall and then immediately traded to the Dallas Mavericks in 1998, Dirk has built a legacy as the greatest player in franchise history. In 12 seasons with the Mavericks, Dirk has averaged 22.9 points and 8.5 rebounds. He's shot 47.8 percent from the floor and an outstanding 38 percent from three-point range. Dirk led Dallas to the only NBA Finals appearance in franchise history in 2006.

His size, agility, and shooting ability make him one of the top inside/outside offensive threats in the league.

It is almost impossible to stop him from scoring one-on-one.

As a nine-time NBA All-Star, a four-time All-NBA First-Team pick, and the 2007 NBA Most Valuable Player, Dirk has set the standard for international players who never played in college in the United States.

When Dirk was 15, his coach told him he had to decide if he wanted to someday play against the best players in the world or simply remain a local hero in his hometown of Würzburg, Germany. For Dirk, the decision was obvious: He went on a vigorous seven-day-a-week training routine that emphasized shooting and passing.

He played for DJK Würzburg of the German Bundesliga and caught the attention of NBA scouts in 1998 at the Nike Hoop Summit. Going against some of the top players his age from the United States, Dirk had 33 points and 14 rebounds.

The rest has become history.

DID YOU KNOW? Dirk created the Dirk Nowitzki Foundation to help fight poverty in Africa.

DIRK NOWITZKI

DERON WILLIAMS
POINT GUARD
UTAH JAZZ

BORN: **6/26/1984**
HEIGHT: **6-3**
WEIGHT: **207 lbs**
SCHOOL: **University of Ilinois**

THE NEW LEGACY

Imagine being Deron Williams. Not only were you the third overall pick in the 2005 NBA Draft, but you were a point guard drafted by a team connected to one of the greatest point guards in history—John Stockton.

Deron, however, has never been intimidated by a challenge: He set out to establish his own legacy as an all-time great point guard. He is already considered by many to be the best playing right now.

In his first season, Deron led the Jazz with 4.5 assists and 10.8 points a game. He was First-Team All-Rookie. But Deron was just getting started. In his second season, he started 80 games and averaged 16.2 points and 9.3 assists, leading the Jazz to the Western Conference Finals in the playoffs.

By the 2007-08 season, Deron was the unquestioned leader of the Jazz. Head coach Jerry Sloan had so much confidence in Deron that he let him call the majority of the Jazz's plays—something he didn't even let John Stockton do.

During the summer of 2008, Deron was selected as a member of "The Redeem Team," which would go on the win back the gold medal for the United States at the Olympics in Beijing, China.

In the 2008-09 season, Deron missed 13 of the first 15 games with an ankle injury, but he still averaged 19.4 points and 10.7 assists. In 2009-10, Deron was finally recognized as a NBA All-Star. Deron also became the first player in NBA history to score at least 20 points and have at least 10 assists in five consecutive playoff games.

So far, his career has been marked by constant improvement. Who knows what the future has in store for this talented player!

DID YOU KNOW? Deron is active in many charities and has his own Points of Hope Foundation, which provides assistance to people with cancer and those who are in need.

DERON WILLIAMS

RAJON RONDO
POINT GUARD
BOSTON CELTICS

BORN: **2/22/1986**
HEIGHT: **6-1**
WEIGHT: **171 lbs**
SCHOOL: **University of Kentucky**

OUT OF THE SHADOWS

Rajon Rondo knows how to handle pressure.

In 2007, he was coming off rookie season during which the Boston Celtics finished 24-58. The Boston Celtics already had All-Star forward Paul Pierce, and they had traded for two more future Hall of Fame players in forward Kevin Garnett and guard Ray Allen.

They were "The Big Three," brought together to win a championship, but even the finest luxury car needs a driver, and Rajon was given the keys. Starting 77 games, Rajon averaged 10.6 points, 5.1 assists, and 4.2 rebounds. The Celtics completed the greatest turnaround in NBA history and went on to capture their first championship since 1986. Rajon didn't get the attention that "The

> Rajon has shown that he is an NBA star, one of the premier point guards in the game. The Boston Celtics' "Big Three" is now the "Big Four."

Big Three" did, but he had gained the respect and confidence of his coaches and teammates.

The next season the Celtics did not return to the Finals, but Rajon averaged 16.9 points, 9.8 assists, and 9.7 rebounds during the Eastern Conference playoffs, and continued his stellar growth last season. He averaged 13.9 points and 9.8 rebounds, and he broke team record for assists in a season held by Hall of Fame point guard Bob Cousy.

But Rajon really emerged from the shadows of the Big Three during the playoffs. He averaged 15.8 points, 9.3 assists, and 5.6 rebounds as the Celtics advanced to the NBA Finals where they lost to the Los Angeles Lakers in a thrilling seven-game series.

DID YOU KNOW? In a game against the Cleveland Cavaliers, Rajon joined Hall of Fame players Wilt Chamberlain and Oscar Robertson as the only players to have 29 points, 18 rebounds, and 13 assists in a playoff game.

RAJON RONDO

STEVE NASH
POINT GUARD
PHOENIX SUNS

BORN: **2/7/1974**
HEIGHT: **6-3**
WEIGHT: **178 lbs**
SCHOOL: **Santa Clara University**

CANADIAN IMPORT

We don't know how good Steve Nash would've been at soccer, but it's hard to imagine he would've been better than he is at basketball. It's a good thing for the NBA that he chose to switch sports!

Steve is not an old-school pass-first guard, nor the modern scoring point guard. He is the perfect blend of both. He can go from playmaker to finisher in the blink of an eye. No matter what action Steve chooses, it usually results in points for his team.

In 14 NBA seasons, Steve has averaged 14.6 points and 8.3 assists. A two-time NBA Most Valuable Player, he joins Magic Johnson and Bob Cousy as the only point guards to win the award. A native of Canada, Steve is also the only Canadian to win MVP.

Looking back, it is amazing that Phoenix fans were not happy when the Suns drafted Steve 15th overall in 1996. He struggled there and was traded to the Dallas Mavericks in 1998. But then something happened. During his six seasons in Dallas, Steve became the top point guard in the league.

He returned to Phoenix as a free agent in 2004 and showed Suns fans what they had missed the first time around. In 2004 and 2005, Steve helped bring the Suns back to prominence and was named MVP. He is one of just 10 players to win back-to-back MVP awards.

Steve is a national hero in Canada for his athletic ability and charitable work. He as been awarded the Order of Canada, which is the highest honor a Canadian citizen can receive. And at the 2010 Winter Olympics in Vancouver, Steve became the first NBA player to participate in the lighting of an Olympic torch.

DID YOU KNOW? Steve Nash supports a lot of great causes including a greener environment. On the Steve Nash Foundation web site, he lists 13 tips for improving the environment and building a healthier community.

STEVE NASH

PAU GASOL
FORWARD/CENTER
LOS ANGELES LAKERS

BORN: **7/6/1980**
HEIGHT: **7-0**
WEIGHT: **250 lbs**

SPANISH SENSATION

It wasn't always obvious that Pau Gasol would be a basketball player. In fact, he started his athletic career in Spain playing rugby, but his love for basketball soon emerged. As he grew, his physical size and athletic ability combined to make him one of the top young stars in all of Europe.

After leading his hometown team FC Barcelona to the Spanish League championship, 20-year-old Pau entered the 2001 NBA Draft. He was selected third-overall by the Atlanta Hawks, but traded to the Memphis Grizzlies. Pau established his NBA credentials quickly by averaging 17.6 points and 8.9 rebounds, making a name for himself as the 2001-02 Rookie of the Year.

Pau's versatility is his strength.

He has the power-game of a 7-footer but also a wide variety of mid-range jumpers. He is extremely difficult to defend. These qualities helped him lead Memphis to three consecutive playoff appearances, after which

Pau was traded to the Los Angeles Lakers in the middle of the 2007-08 season.

With All-Star Kobe Bryant as his teammate, he became the first citizen of Spain to reach the NBA Finals. The Lakers lost to the Boston Celtics, but Pau wasn't about to give up. The next season he made his second All-Star team and the Lakers returned to the Finals—and this time, they won. He was an All-Star again in 2010, and the Lakers repeated as champions, defeating the Celtics and avenging the 2008 loss.

In addition to his on court performances for the NBA, Pau is also proud to represent Spain in FIBA basketball tournaments. In 2006, he was named MVP of the FIBA World Championships and led Spain to its first title. Pau also won a silver medal for Spain at the 2008 Olympics and a gold medal at the 2009 European Championships. He was named FIBA Europe Player of the Year in 2009 and 2010.

DID YOU KNOW? Pau was a student at the medical school at the University of Barcelona before he decided to pursue a professional basketball career. He remains interested in medicine and often visits the Children's Hospital of Los Angeles.

PAU GASOL

DERRICK ROSE
POINT GUARD
CHICAGO BULLS

BORN: **10/4/1988**
HEIGHT: **6-3**
WEIGHT: **190 lbs**
SCHOOL: **University of Memphis**

HOMETOWN HERO

Chicago has been waiting. A decade of glory led by the great Michael Jordan brought the Windy City six NBA titles during the 1990s, but since Jordan retired in 1997, the Bulls have waited for a star to replace him.

Who knew that player was growing up on the south side of Chicago during those glory years? Derrick won two state championships at Chicago's Simeon Career Academy before going on to star at the University of Memphis. After leading the Tigers to the NCAA Championship game as a freshman, Derrick entered the 2008 NBA Draft. The Bulls had the No. 1 overall pick in the draft and wasted no time selected their hometown prodigy. Derrick did not disappoint.

As a player with the skills of both a point and scoring guard, Derrick understands how to make the difficult transition from playmaker to scorer during a game. In his first 10 games as a Bull, he became the first player since Michael Jordan to score at least 10 points. He joined Michael and Elton Brand as the only Bulls to be named NBA Rookie of the Year. The Bulls then made the playoffs and Derrick tied an NBA record for a rookie record by scoring 36 in his playoff debut.

In 2009-10, Derrick became the first Bull to make the All-Star team since Michael in 1998, and Chicago returned to the playoffs. It seems like it could only be a matter of team before Derrick leads the Bulls to a NBA title, just like Mike.

DID YOU KNOW? In his playoff debut, Derrick Rose scored 36 points and dished 11 assists against the Boston Celtics. He is only the second player in NBA history to score at least 35 points and have 10 assists in his first playoff game, joining Chris Paul.

DERRICK ROSE

TIM DUNCAN
FORWARD
SAN ANTONIO SPURS

BORN: 4/25/1976
HEIGHT: 6-11
WEIGHT: 260 lbs
SCHOOL: Wake Forest University

MR. CONSISTENCY

The best stars are the ones that never lose their brightness. In 1997, Tim Duncan entered the NBA as one of the best basketball players in the world and he still is one of the best.

In 13 NBA seasons, Tim is a 12-time All-Star; he has been named First Team All-NBA nine times, the NBA Most Valuable Player in 2002 and 2003, and was 1998's Rookie of the Year. But most importantly, Tim has led the Spurs to NBA titles in 1999, 2003, 2005, and 2007. He was MVP of the Finals three times.

His precision skills have earned him the nickname "The Big Fundamental."

He may not look flashy, but he always gets the job done. His trademark is a mid-range bank shot—not a dunk. Tim has said, "If you show excitement, then you may also show disappointment or frustration. If your opponent picks up on this frustration, you are at a disadvantage."

By averaging 21.1 points, 11.6 rebounds, and 2.3 blocks and winning four titles, Tim is one of the greatest power forwards in history.

He has played his entire career in San Antonio, never leaving for a bigger city or brighter spotlight. Besides San Antonio, it appears the only other place where Tim's star will shine will be in Springfield, Mass., at the Naismith Memorial Basketball Hall of Fame.

DID YOU KNOW? Growing up in St. Croix, Virgin Islands, Tim wanted to be an Olympic swimmer. When Hurricane Hugo destroyed the country's only Olympic-sized pool in 1989, the team had to train by swimming in the ocean. He stopped because he was afraid of sharks!

TIM DUNCAN

AMAR'E STOUDEMIRE
FORWARD/CENTER
NEW YORK KNICKS

BORN: 11/16/1982
HEIGHT: 6-10
WEIGHT: 249 lbs
SCHOOL: Cypress Creek (Fla.) High School

BIG APPLE'S BIG PLAYER

If Amar'e Stoudemire was looking for a stage to showcase his skills, he could not have picked a bigger one.

After spending the first eight years of his NBA career with the Phoenix Suns, Amar'e will begin the 2010-11 season with the New York Knicks.

He is the centerpiece in what all of New York hopes will be the rebirth of Knicks basketball. One player cannot win a title by himself, but Amar'e, with his powerful play around the basket, is a great player for the Knicks to position for their title chase.

Amar'e did not start playing organized basketball until he was 14, but immediately showed he had the potential to be a star. He entered the 2002 NBA Draft straight after high school graduation and was selected by Phoenix with the 9th overall pick.

Amar'e averaged 13.5 points and 8.8 rebounds to become the first player drafted from high school to be named NBA Rookie of the Year. The next year, with Amar'e averaging a team-high 26 points, the Suns won 62 games and he made his first All-Star team.

Things were falling into place for the young athlete. But the 2005-06 season proved to be a difficult one. Amar'e had to have knee surgery in the preseason and only played three games that season. Many wondered if he would be the same great player when he returned.

Amar'e erased all doubts when he played all 82 games and averaged 20.4 points and 9.6 rebounds in 2006-07. He made his second straight All-Star team and was All-NBA First-Team. Amar'e was having another great season in 2008-09 when an eye injury forced him to miss the final 29 games of the season. But once again he triumphed over the naysayers when he returned to average 23.1 points and 8.9 rebounds in 2009-10. He made his fifth straight All-Star team—and he's hoping to repeat the performance in New York.

DID YOU KNOW? Amar'e is known as "STAT" (Standing Tall And Talented). He won a 2008 NBA Community Assist Award.

AMAR'E STOUDEMIRE

Each season they entertain us with their incredible skills, but some players reach a level that truly sets them apart. Not just superstars, but MEGASTARS.

Each of them has his own story to greatness.

Now you know how and why these players became the best of the best in the National Basketball Association.